flowers and philosophies

flowers and philosophies

ISBN: 978-1-71663-130-6

Lulu Publishing

www.karinatavares.com

Published and printed in the United States of America 2020

to my dearest readers,

these mini stories, these poems you're about to read are the words that came in rushing from my head to my hands sprinkling like stardust across these pages to bring you this collection.

thank you so much for allowing me to live my dream.

now, as you flip through these pages do it slowly, savor every word, imagine every moment as if it were your own because as much as this is my story it is also yours.

let me take your heart out for a spin.

i hope this book inspires you.

welcome to book number three.

this is flowers and philosophies and she is magic.

"but i need to feel beautiful and holy things around me, always: music, mystery cults, symbols, myths. i need it, and i refuse to give it up that's my fatal flaw."

--hermann hesse, damian

flowers and philosophies playlist:

(a list of the songs that were playing while i was writing this book)

for the ultimate experience play these songs in order in the background while reading this book

dreams -- nuages

cruel world -- active child

house of cards -- radio head

so hot you're hurting my feelings -- caroline polachek

two out of three ain't bad -- meatloaf

cosmic freeway -- yeek

dorian -- agnes obel

anchor -- novo amor

dancing with your ghost -- sasha sloan

run cried the crawling -- agnes obel

talk show host -- radio head

i'm god -- clams casino

cosmic flower -- levitation room

i am a wild flower that grew
on the side of the road,

i am the flesh of the full moon,
a pile of old and worn books,

i take beauty tips from 400 year old
red wood trees and torn down
marble and stone temples.

i have more preservation than a jar of
homemade dark red cherry jam,

and

my soul is a sword made of silver and gold,

it is the song of rebellion and triumph,
and it is as sweet as river water.

i am curiosity and wonder,
laughter and rain,

and yet

i have stood the test of time,
and pain,
and growth,

and here i am.

this is me.
this is my song.

[karina's song]

beware of the girl

brushing her hair

in the mirror,

and

of the false sense of danger
in her solitude.

[in my thirst i’ve learned that hell hath no fury]

a feeling
a melodic awakening

blooming like spring,
ripe like peaches in the summer.

so ripe like when you take a bite
and it's so ripe the juice drips down
your hands and arms,

it becomes sticky, annoying
you're done with it,
you've eaten it through the core.

throw away the pit, wash your hands clean.

let's forget how it takes a whole season for
the peaches to ripen, to bloom again

how it takes its time to grow and to be wonderful
for you to just throw it away like you never really
liked peaches anyway,

like you never loved me anyway.

[peaches part one]

when a boy compares you to a peach
sometimes he doesn't know that your
rosy cheeks and velvet skin
can bruise easy like

peaches.

sweet like candy, ready to be eaten up

or

left to rot.

not knowing that inside you carry the
heaviest seed that is sometimes left behind
or even worse,

thrown away.

not knowing that if you plant it,
it'll grow and grow
into something beautiful
with a lingering sweetness.

but you will never know because
you never loved me...
or
not like *peaches,* anyway.

[peaches part two]

my mind is the view of a mountain
that i have yet to climb.

calm.
focused.
still.
wondering.

everything becomes silent,
and i see my life pass right before my eyes
i realized that my life was a vast, glowing
empty page and i was the creator.

i am the pen, the paintbrush,
i am the magicians fingers.

i could be or do anything i wanted,
all i needed to do was want it bad enough.

[when did we stop believing in magic?]

bruised and tender

a lot like the fruit
no one picks up
at the fruit market.

like the fruit that has been dropped too
many times and has taken a few more punches
than the rest.

the one that's not as pretty,
shiny,
or as spotless
as the rest but nonetheless
it's still a fruit.

it's bruising doesn't make it any less sweet
or any less ripe
because when you cut it open,
right in half,

it has its core, it's still whole.

just like the rest.

[traumatic experiences don't define you]

note to self: all you do is drink and cry.

note to self: you are *stronger* than vodka
and sparkling water.

note to self: they asked if you're okay again
and you said yes...

you've become the biggest liar.

the worst part?

not to them, but to yourself.

[these notes to self are becoming so repetitive:
openness they say, will finally set you free]

have you ever craved human interaction so much that it *physically hurts?*

all my life i've valued flowers and books over cars and careers.

and now here i am,

i am so fucking lonely living in a world where every single person is just so *plugged in.*

where no one wants to disconnect to *connect...*

to each other.

it's like a video game i want out of because no matter what i do or say i will always be ill-equipped to lose, every time.

i want the REAL world.

trees, air, soil, mind and body,

are you as lonely as me living in this world?

tell me i am not the only one.

i CRAVE interaction like a drug addict.

I CRAVE IT.

but you just can't anymore

because i wasn't made for a world that treats you like a machine,

a world where money, jobs, a fancy suit, arrogant content and god-like blazed illusions is the motive--

where the false world has become the real world.
where material possessions are valued more than the ethical, the moral, the good.

tell me, when will the madness stop.

when will we stop letting consumerism, consume us,
when will we stop letting the things we own,
own us.

when will we put our devices down to just breathe.

let us be kind,
let us not be darkened by a fantasy anymore.

[flowers and philosophies—a girl with a utopian dream]

REMINDER FROM YOUR HIGHER SELF: read a good book today, pour yourself a glass of even better wine and don't forget to look at the moon every once in a while.

after every single one of my relationships
it felt like i became a watered down version
of myself.

it felt like i was coming home from war.

torn down,
like,
i was still *me*
but
something inside of me was broken,
stolen.

i never came back home the same after war,
or should i say,

after you.

[after]

if i could relive any moment

forever,

over and over again

it would be:

morning sunshine on your face through
that hotel window.

[showered in sunlight]

once upon a time i painted a portrait in my mind of a golden field of flowers and of a man that is the silver shield that reflects *me*.

there is grass and breeze,
and a home with the scent of spice,
sweet nectar and *love.*

we created our own world within the wildflowers we planted on the side of our yard.

our story,
is *everywhere.*

it is in the songs we hum in the bright purple skies at sunset,

it is in the bristles of grass that tickle our feet as we drift away hand in hand into our secret lake

where they can't see us,
or touch us,

because we can barely hear them where we are,

because it's just us.

in this moment.

in our world.

in our secret lake dancing beneath the stars with just the light of the moon illuminating our bodies as we become one over and over again.

[our secret]

the first moment,
the very first moment our eyes got locked
into a *gaze,*

we drowned in love.

we never forced it,
we couldn't explain it.

all i know is that for some reason your chemicals
and my chemicals want each other,

desperately,
since the very first day.

that's what i love the most about us.

[i forget about time and space but i can't stop
thinking about your face]

all my life i've heard that your heart is always
right and that if you follow it you will always
find your way.

ever since then i've shut off my mind
and listened to my heart.

for years i've followed its rhythm and beats
like my map of life.

emotions over logic.
passionate about everything.

and most importantly,

no. more. lukewarm. love.

[the power of love will change your life]

when i was a little girl, i read a book about wolves. it taught me that a wolf retreats to a dark place when it's wounded to recover,

or die alone.

but i am no wolf and neither are you because untreated pain is a cancer that will kill you,

soul first.

untreated pain will eat you through the core,
and you will sit there with your wound wide open,
trying to shove whatever it is to stop the pain and the trauma from bursting out of you like fireworks.

[remember that it's okay to ask for help, remember that you will heal one day and you don't need to over drink, or over medicate yourself even if it feels like you're drowning. you are more than the worst thing that has ever happened to you]

if it's true,
that the eyes are the windows to the soul
then i would like to keep my window *closed,*

because my soul is *broken,*
beaten,

and this window is only made up of an abyss
of sorrow and way too many regrets.

[i wrote this at a very sad time in my life. i wanted to let you know that it's okay to feel sad sometimes. i know what it feels like. take a deep breath today and remember that you are loved] dandelions are my favorite.

they might not be everyone's first choice,

they are not the flower of choice for a lover to show their affection,

nor are they the ones you pick out at your local flower shop to decorate your house with,

their petals aren't as soft as the ones on roses,

or

the ones you squeeze to use their sweet aroma as perfume or to bathe in.

i know they probably aren't the best to look at.

but,

they're my favorite because they are
free and *wild* ...

but most importantly, they can't ever be *bought*.

[as i stared into the open field, the sweet aroma of spring hit me, i was fixated on a group of dandelions]

TIPS FOR RADIANT SKIN: question authority, read more books, be kind, sit in nature alone and bathe in rainbows and flowers.

i ask the universe about happiness and i get a
sunset or a sunrise in my favorite colors.

sometimes in purples and pinks with hues of orange.

some days i have a heart full of sadness and the
universe sends me a stormy sky.

a rainy, cloudy day to be in solidarity with me.

sometimes i ask about the meaning of life and i get
a flower in pure bloom.

the universe decides to cover me in trees,
to bathe me in nature.

my answers were always there,
i just needed to listen carefully,
not with my *ears* but with my *heart*.

[all the answers are within you]

i don't know how to look at your skin
and not think of home.

the way you smell reminds me more of home and of
"i've been here before…"
than my childhood home *times four.*

i fit so effortlessly into your arms that i can't
help but feel in my heart that it's where i belong

forever.

i don't know how to look at your skin
and not think of home because only in
your arms did i realize that home for me
was not a place,

it was the longing in my heart
for you.

[i could just die in your arms and melt away all of
my existence and then melt right into you instead]

advice to my younger self from my older self:

don't worry if someone is mean to you. if their hurtful words ever get to you just be the bigger person. LITERALLY become so much bigger than them by devouring their souls until you're double or triple their size.

even when i forget for a while i'm reminded.

"what's that accent?"
"you're not from here, right?"

because even if for a second i dare to forget
i'm reminded need with words like--

"exotic"

"where are you really from?"

and my personal favorite,

"you've been *randomly* selected."

because even if i drape myself in hundreds and
thousands of different flags i will never feel
warm *enough.*

because i've always been reminded that my
grandparents and my parents journey is far
from over.

an immigrants journey is never over.

but as i look in the mirror, i'm reminded that
these two brown eyes has carried the desert that
my ancestors once walked through...

my blood, the same that my people carried through
their veins, it's as rich as the juice of a
thousand cherries.

and this heart,

it's a heart that beats just like the drums that my people danced to for thousands of years.

my people ruled like gods,
sung and danced to the sun,
and the moon,
they fought like warriors.

a precious gift that has been passed on from generation to generation until this very moment right here,

right now,
that sits in my eyes, my hair, in the depths of my skin and veins but most importantly it's here...

here in this beating heart,

so that if you forget,

for even a second...

you're reminded.

[an immigrants story]

i started to write poems and books because i
wanted to spread happiness like a wildfire.

i wanted to heal and comfort the world.

but not with stupid little poems about the
sky being blue and the ocean being vast.

i wanted to be raw and honest.
i wanted to show you my battle scars.

i wanted to show you authenticity in a world that
is lackluster, a world that's turned on by the
false,

my pen became my sword
and my heart became my gift to you.

i knew that if i wanted to write the way i wanted
to i needed to reopen every wound i spent years
closing.

my wounds had to be re-opened slowly,
stitch by stitch they became unhinged like a flower
silently screaming as its petals are being ripped
off from its core,

it's always been writing vs feelings.

you look at me and you might see a poet writing a
book... but if you look a little closer,

it's a war.

[nobody said it was going easy, but nobody said it
would hurt this much]

at sixteen i learned what cruel meant,
when a monster with ragged breath
and with a fever to destroy innocence
decided that it was okay to force himself onto me
and to shatter my porcelain skin and crack my soul
to pieces like twigs that break under hunters feet.

ever since then,
i taught myself to keep my teeth sharpened,
like a crown of thorns,
hidden beneath a broken smile,
because you never know
when you'll need to bite your way out
of a beast that has swallowed you whole.

[at sixteen my life as i knew it changed forever]

is there a drink deep enough to drown in?

is there a quiet enough to live in?

because my hands are raw from scrubbing my regrets
i keep stumbling and falling,
i keep drowning in the same water
i learned to swim in years ago.

[i was not born to keep drowning like this]

when you first found out you were so excited.
at that point i was genderless, i was a mere speck of life and you-
dad,
cried tears of joy because at your age and after trying so many times you thought it was impossible.

you loved me when you didn't know whether i was going to be a boy or a girl.

after months of waiting you finally found out i was going to be girl.

there wouldn't be enough swords in the world for you to defend your little girl, since the day i was born you tried to defend me from everything, but certain things destiny had already set in stone like me being born a *girl.*

one day, you knew i had to go out into the world by myself.

you knew that there were things you wouldn't be able to defend me from even if you tried.

like when i started high school,
like when the boys in my class started to classify girls and their hands started to wander without asking permission...

all i could think about was how could the same gender as the person who always tried to protect me could be so cruel.

were you like the boys in my school dad?

i need to know if you called the girls in your
class bitches and sluts too,
i need to know if your hands wandered too.

tell me, did you treat them like a something
instead of a someone like how the boys treated
me, dad?

please tell me that not all men are created equal,
tell me you were different.

dad, did you ever regret me being born a girl?

when you first found out,
when i was a mere speck of life with no gender,

you loved me.

you even cried tears of joy.

but,

when you found out i was going to be born a girl,
i changed your world.

[another 'dear dad' poem]

wealth to me was never about money.
being wealthy always meant to me something more,
something that came from inside.

wealth meant happiness.
if i'm happy i'm rich.
if i'm happy i'm the wealthiest person alive.

i look up at the stars while laying in the grass,
barefoot and with the cool night wind gently
caressing my face and i can't help to think...

"i've never been richer."

[i like it here, where the flowers sing me
lullabies, it was here where i found my freedom]

let's play a game—

put a flower in your hair every time someone tells you can't have fun all the time.

put a flower in your hair every time someone tells you to "stop dressing that way."

put a flower in your hair every time someone tells you "that's impossible."

put a flower in your hair for every dream you have.

just keep putting flowers in your hair until you become a beautiful garden. you are now free.

[let them keep talking, you just keep looking up at the clouds, keep collecting your flowers, keep being you, your dreams are worth it, you are beautiful] i've known you before.

that was my first reaction when we first met.

i can't quite explain it, but the first time i looked into your eyes i knew i've seen them before. it was the feeling of "you've known me" and "i've known you" for *centuries.*

it wasn't a physical attraction or chemical, but an attraction from a different *dimension.*

a *soul-traction.*

like our souls have been intertwined before,

like if my atoms picked your atoms when we were just merely stardust,

because i now understand every 11:11 and 4:44 that led me straight to you.

my 7 suns,

my divinity,

my souls secret.

a language that could be only spoken between our locked gaze, our hidden language between the flutter of our eyelashes.

i'm finally home.

[11:11]

i'm convinced by now that my heart only
beats for you.

it only knows your name.

the day we locked eyes my heart went wild,

i wasn't expecting that, my heart wasn't
expecting *this...*

it doesn't know about distance or time
all it knows is *you,*

we could spend years apart,
and i know i'll always go back to you.

years could pass by,
and i know i'll love you the same.

i'll always be ready to pick up right where we
left off,

years could pass by and i'll still want you
for the rest of my life.

[some things aren't meant to be understood, only
lived like my love for you]

i like sleeping next to you...
no wait, scratch that

i absolutely *love* sleeping next to you.

the way we touch each other
the way our hands fit so seamless into one another
and the warmth of our naked bodies
together in a bond, knotted close,
every curve of my body filled in with yours,
with your skin and your hands,

my defenses are down
our breath becomes one
a wave of love so deep fills me up.

"you mean more to me than you'll ever know."
"there aren't any words."

as you lay on my chest and you close your eyes you
listen to my heart.

"i trust you with all my soul."

i close my eyes too.

[do you ever wish you could frame a moment in time
just like a picture?]

your love tastes like my favorite red wine
with cherries at the bottom.

your touch is like the velvet glove of a patient lover.

and your eyes...

my god.

those fucking eyes could swallow every star and universe i had living inside of me.

one look at you and i knew you were going to be the death of me.

[you killed me i'm so in love with you]

she is hell fire and cherry bark.

ash and embers,

she is a fire that burns,
in the middle of a blizzard.

she is your eden,
signed with a bullet.

she is your highest high and your everything
all at once.

her heart is a clenched fist that slowly opened up
its ravenous mouth,

it's an open cage for you to sleep in.

*"lay your tongue over the fire if you want to know
what i taste like..."*

you lick the ash off your fingers.

*hell hath no fury
hell hath no fury*
...

[they all want a strong woman until they meet a
strong woman]

and how could i not be *soft*
with a hint of a dark side personality...

when i have hope and rage living inside of me,

intertwined,
interconnected,
like two gods fighting till death for the power of
whom gets to live inside of my head.

one tastes like cold rain water
across my parched mouth...

it does the trick.
for now at least.

the other is a honey-trap, or a venus fly trap that
lets me stand on its center and it lets me peak
inside,

it lets me believe that i touched bliss
until it closed its mouth
and swallowed me whole...

leaving me empty inside.

[chaos makes the muse]

this tragedy rocked me
back
and
forth.

for years.

and it has become *exhausting* to act stronger
than what i really am.

keeping up the act has become my own mental prison.

no one ever tells you how messy healing truly is.

so here i am with all my broken pieces,

here are my shambles and my stirred spirit,

here i am with my *openness,*

my greatest weapon.

[in the midst of your darkness you will find that
your light is your greatest weapon]

be proud of every scar on your body,
it's an autograph signed by you for your
strength and willingness to continue in this world.

wear your scars like metals and merits
you've won for your bravery.

[only you understand the violence it took to become this gentle]

the following is an actual excerpt from a journal entry from when i was seventeen years old.

**names and small details were changed for privacy reasons.*

date: some spring day in 2008

age: 17

time: 2:00 pm

i had survived my suicide attempt and as much as everybody around me was trying to make things *"normal"* again for me it was only making things weird and awkward. my parents wanted to pretend it never happened except when i would go to the bathroom and they thought i never noticed them spying on me or how now my bedroom door had to remain open at all times and as if that wasn't bad enough dr. H, my therapist was considering "group therapy" because she thought it would be good for me. i don't know if i secretly hated dr. H for this and i came to therapy as a need to fulfill my sadistic ways or if i only came to her therapy sessions because she always had a great selection of assorted candies in that ugly ass ceramic bowl. i spent like half of our 45 minutes together chewing mini snickers and caramels anyway. the other half i spent drawing my feelings and doing breathing exercises about lemons. yes, fucking lemons. i told myself that if she ever ran out of candies i wouldn't ever come back.

date: another spring day in 2008

age: 17

time: 10:30 am

the following is a recording from one of my sessions with dr. H.

me: "why?" "why shouldn't i be allowed to feel this way or why should i give life another shot?"

dr. H: "people are concerned." "your mother brought you here because she cares."

me: "cares?"

me: "you really believe that?"

[my thoughts: it was like hearing her read right out of a therapy for dummies handbook. it was like a 'i just want to clock out and go home' kind of an answer.]

me: "do you really believe people can care about each other?"

me: "or do we treat people with compassion because we feel bad for them? i don't want people to be compassionate with me because i don't deserve it. i'm not compassionate."

[theres a long pause. at this point i'm crying and as much as i wanted to believe therapy wasn't for me or that it wasn't working, i had one of many breakthroughs that day.]

[page 42 continued]

me: "i have no respect for my father because he is just bossed around by my mother at this point, even though she has basically dedicated her life to taking care of him during his illness."

me: "not only do i hate her for her "compassion" but i resent her because it's interfering with my life."

me: "and as fucked up as that sounds... i love her for her compassion because that night she found me in my room with those twenty-eight pills in my hand, before I could do anything else she stopped me..."

me: "do you know what that means dr. H?"

me: "if it wasn't because of that act of compassion, i wouldn't even be here today."

end.

it's funny how a lot of people call my poetry art,
when in reality it was a cry for help.

[i'm sorry for the mess]

most people would prefer to be the lamb
over the beast.

but you should never fear the existence of either
growing inside of you.

it is important to have an equal balance of both.

for it takes the innocence of the lamb and the
heart of the beast to gather perspective.

do not be afraid to speak up.

your voice is yours,
so you should always speak with it.

your arms and legs might tremble, but remember
they're only shaking hard enough for you to take
flight.

even if you trip at the finish line,
you still made it.

you are not your mothers child or your fathers
disappointment,

you are now the sun in your own solar system, you
have your own gravity.

do not shut it off,
instead let it pull you in on all things good.

[sunscreen 2.0]

i remember that even as a child i was always utterly obsessed with the planets.

my favorite was the moon.

the moon always looked the most beautiful to me when it was full.

i would day dream and pretend the moon was a disco ball in the sky and the stars were the glittering reflections of it and the world i was standing on was my dance floor and i was just dancing away in this human realm.

don't stop dreaming and don't stop believing in magic; child you needs you to hold on to some of that magic you once believed in.

[don't let the world create a watered down dulled version of you]

growing up is never growing older.
it is growing sweeter and perhaps wiser.

[don’t grow up it’s a trap]

the smell of lavender and mint.
the taste of chamomile tea and honey.

the song and vibrations of people and nature
swimming together and blending in as seamless as
watercolours.

i can feel myself placing a bookmark

here,

in this moment in time.

[my thoughts while looking out my window this
morning]

let me remember the taste of youth and the smell of
every summer i've spent sipping on dreams. i want
to remember the taste of life dancing in my lungs.

i want to feel the warmth of sunlight on my skin
over and over again.

[childhood dreams]

when you learn to forgive yourself,
something awakens within you.

when you bring yourself to tears of deep healing,

when your breath begins to align
with your heartbeat,

when you begin to treat yourself with
respect,
kindness,
gentleness.

when you learn to forgive every past version
of yourself,
for the darkness,
the pain,
the sorrow,

healing is the process of
falling back into love
with yourself.

so break down,
rebuild,
heal,
rise.

[the human experience]

they say the dark only arises
to give in room for the light.

so until the moon is full again,
i'll sow my tears here,

into the darkness of the night.

until day arrives,
and the sun wraps me
back up into its comforting warmth,

until i am able to bloom again.

[rebirth]

did you ever hear that saying how every time a butterfly flaps its wings it causes a hurricane?

or in other words, have you ever heard of *'the butterfly effect theory?'*

how every action no matter how small can have a cause and effect on everything?

how every choice you've ever made, even what shirt you decided to wear today,

led you to this moment,
right here,
right now.

so are we in control?

are we really?

if in one blink,
with just one choice,

we can cause a hurricane.

[the butterfly effect]

nature has always been the only thing that
could ever soften my rough edges,

it slows me back down,
bringing me to a standstill,
making me blurry. even,
like birds could fly right through me,

and maybe they do...

my god, i hope they do.

[the place between real and surreal is where i always wish to remain] here's the picture:

two strangers in a closed room and the only way they get to communicate and get to know each other is through their favorite songs.

these are the things no one ever told you about
self love,

like when i look in the mirror and i think:

"if only i could see you through the eyes of a
stranger... then maybe, i could love myself."

because through my eyes all i see is a battered,
broken down body with bones too heavy to carry,

through my eyes my body is terror and bruises.

but through your eyes my body is whole.

through your eyes my body is capable of love.

so give me your eyes
so that maybe,
one day,
i could see what you see in me.

give me your eyes so i could learn to love me,
the way you love me.

[i think i love myself]

career goal: heavens full moon or the gleam in your eye when you're doing something you love, sometimes i can't even tell the difference.

i promise to always choose the taste of love over
fear against my tongue;

i promise i will choose the beauty of life and its
fragrant flowers,

so that i may have a place to hide
from the darkness of my mind
and its savage forests,

so that i may always have a safe place to undress
my mind and untangle my soul.

[may you find your haven, may you find your peace]

you can die many metaphorical times in life,

like for example, the first time i ever died was when i loved someone else more than i ever loved myself.

to love, to feel, to touch without giving all of myself is a foreign concept to me.

the truth is i am as full of destruction
as i am affection.

you crave the sensation of me on top of you,
but you do not understand me.

do not be fooled by the kindness in my eyes or the softness of my skin-

i am a multitude of miraculous tragedies dressed in art.

as much as i want to love you and spread the deepest parts of myself over you like the tides on a coastal shore,

i know you cannot love me in the way that i demand to be loved.

you are too accustomed to the idea of affection
with no lasting consequence.

and so...

you cannot possibly have enough to give without
leaving me at least somewhat empty.

i am someone full of presence-
and any absence you leave
will
leave
me

BARE.

[love is too dangerous for people like me]

the butterflies you gave me colored the warm air
when we first met then they even learned how to
play jump rope with the veins and cords in my heart
until one day you clipped their wings with your
lies and now i can no longer feel their effect.

[the butterfly effect]

sometimes when i put the windows down in my car i like to pretend that the wind is just your hands in my hair.

an old soul.

a label that was pinned to me at a very young age.

but the older i do get i began to suspect that i am
not very old at all.

from the way i stare at each sunset in utter
wonderment and joy,

and the intrigue that hums through my body at the
sight of flowers and artworks.

the older i do get i have began to realize that
it's actually quite possible that i'm one of the
youngest souls there is...

for what a fortune it is to see everything like
it's the first time.

[redefine old soul]

you survived.

you didn't think you would ever make it to twenty-two let alone twenty-eight.

seventeen and a fist full of pills and a soul full of sorrow.

and yet you survived.

you fell in love.

you wrote books like those authors you always admired.

you got that record player you always wanted.

you got all of those tattoos you wanted.

it's been more than a decade here,

you survived and you are still surviving.

[my heart will always break for seventeen year old me i just want to go back in time and whisper in her ear... "give life one more chance, it'll be worth your while, *just trust me...*"]

the bravest thing i ever did was continuing my life
even when i wanted it to end.

[seventeen]

i always knew that if the end of the world happened
i would go looking for you.

every. single. time.

i would want to die in your arms and take my last
breath into your mouth...

[and yet i know the feeling isn't mutual, and yet i
would still go look for you and that will never
change]

i am tired of your touch telling me that i am hard to love just because you didn't expect to find the coldness that runs down my spine that makes me shiver and run every time you touch it.

you didn't expect to find pin holes inside my soul
you didn't expect eyes that leak like broken faucets.

you hate the pitter patter and now you know what it meant when i told you one book ago to *imagine what the ocean could do to a girl like me...*

this is what it's like to swim in the middle of my ocean. the water is sometimes warm but dark. it's silent but from time to time you could hear a soft hum going off into the horizon.

i'm sorry my hands never instructed yours on how to hold me without breaking or burning.

i'm sorry you never learned how to swim in my ocean.

[damaged goods]

SAGITTARIUS: how come you never seem to be as good at building the bridge as you are burning it?

ever since you left every mountain i paint
looks upsettingly cold.

like if certain items could kill you if you
had to climb it.

others with a view you wish you could wake up to.

all they were missing was your name.

["you remind me of the colour blue"]

how to unlove you:

slowly.

painfully.

very painfully.

i grew a new heart and a new soul that this time around could not be corrupted by you.

around my heart i made sure to grow translucent crystals imprisoned within cold ice.

exquisitely strong,

with no regrets.

["the interlude"]

wear your wounds like wings.

have you ever felt like some sleep deprived intern
of the universe accidentally put the soul of a
small soft white moth into your human body and then
all of a sudden you're here in this big bad world
sitting by lamps and resting close to fires
wondering why you feel out of place at school and
at the mall...

[the big blunder]

my
heart
will
always
be
a
broken
wonderland.

have you ever been or seen one of those penthouse parties?

you know...

those huge penthouse parties with a pool in the backyard filled with random strangers partying away

a beautiful view.

but there are no photos on the wall, no warm cooked meals being cooked in the kitchen, no clothes hanging from the closet...

all it is, is a beautiful place for strangers to come in for a while and then leave.

you might think to yourself: "it must be pretty lonely when the party is over."

i was that empty room. that empty penthouse.

left all alone, in the cold, in the dark.

but today i have promised myself to be a *home.*
no more strangers and no more empty cold rooms.

remember to always fill your life with the right people. people that will truly love you. don't let strangers use you and leave you after the party is over.

your body is a treasure and your mind is a gold mine. fill yourself with love, warmth and especially kindness.

turn yourself into a home, not an empty penthouse.

[build a home out of yourself]

a deer goes for a drink and sees the reflection of a tiger in the water.

[perception]

there are two types of relationships in life:

those that inspire us to give out our best life and then there are those that... destroy us.

there are those that gives us peace and those that take it away,

and yet even while knowing this we always continue to choose wrong.

every. single. time.

why do we time after time choose the type of love that destroys us? the one that tears us apart.

society and its stereotypes pushes us toward that chaos. it teaches us that pain is fun when it is anything but.

pain is perverse.

pain is exciting.

but most of all, it hurts.

we kill what we love to only suffocate with a foreign lung that was never enough for two people.

we are left gasping for air because a love worth dying for is the formula we've tattooed on our souls for far too long.

[why do we kill what we love]

i'm tired of being fed the type of love that messes with my head and turns me into shit.

a love that despairs,

and exasperates.

i'm tired of the type of love that hurts, that feels worth dying for, that drains my spirit leaving me breathless.

i'm tired of not being loved with tenderness.

or kindness.

loneliness bites the soul and disdain cuts the skin. such is life. i just never knew that when they said love kills that it was more than just a metaphor of corny stupid words together...

love, if not given the right or correct dose will eat you alive. soul first. love kills. literally.

[nobody else is hurt by oblivion]

writing saved my life. it still saves me.
when i write i don't exist.

even if it's just for a little while.

when my tears can't stop falling i know i can write
until my edges start to blur and my words start to
blend with my tears like watercolour on a canvas.

i can start feeling less...
less real,
less solid,
lighter even.

i begin to find the rip in the tide of the world
and i begin to let myself get swept away by it.

i begin to be filled by peaceful nothingness as
those three little dots roll onto the end of my
sentence like three sweet little blueberries

...

and oh how i salivate for them every day.

[a fire that can melt the world]

how stupid of me to try and plant a garden of beautiful flowers inside of your chest when your heart was just an empty cave and it never had the fertile soil i needed to plant my garden.

[the flower bloomed and faded, the sun rose and sank, the lover loved and left]

two books ago i compared you to a drug...
in human form.

i told you how your high hit quick and i always
wanted to come back for more.

i told you, you were *lethal.*

two books ago i told you how you were my favorite
drug of choice,

but here's the thing about drugs...

they wear off.

[two books later and you've finally worn off]

i remember the time when you told me “we should see other people” and how my heart was completely shattered... i still remember how in that moment i wanted to be someone, anyone but myself so then maybe you could fall in love with me all over again.

[even if i had told you i still loved you in a million different ways it wouldn't of changed a thing because i was still me]

it wasn't like a bang of explosives,
there weren't any fireworks,

it was slow and gentle,

it was like someone lighting a candle in a dark room and a soft light immediately over powers the darkness.

this is what your love felt like.

[thank you for pouring your gentle love inside of me thank you for calming the war i had inside]

i used to live off air until my lips touched love
for the very first time.

[i thought air was all you needed to live until the
swirling ache of love and loss made a home inside
of my chest]

when i think of the scariest thing that can ever happen to me, it is to have taken away the thing i love the most.

[you]

i loved you

and you...

never loved me.

i loved you and you knew that's all it would be.

you took me to the edge and pushed me off.

i loved you and that's all it ever was,

me loving you and you *leaving me.*

[i am sorry for believing it could have been any other way]

this is who i am:

i am a woman who has known great pains

but also great happiness.

i am a woman who has known pleasure

but also sorrow.

i am a woman that has had to make hard choices,
but i followed my heart every step of the way.

i am a woman that survived so i could thrive.

[to be a woman]

have you ever had a really vivid dream where you live an entire life from beginning to end and then you wake up, breathless, still foggy eyed and feeling so overwhelmingly... *homesick?*

[i have lived ten lifetimes since last night]

ADVICE FROM YOUR HIGHER SELF: read good books and drink even better wine it's an emergency!

to feel grounded: place your hands onto the soil.

to heal yourself: float slowly in river water.

to recharge: relax your shoulders and raise your face to the beaming rays of the sun.

to reclaim your power: run a salt bath and bathe under the full moon. let the moonlight make a home out of your soul.

[attached to nothing, connected to everything]

NOTE TO SELF: make something out of your memories
remember that your pain is as good and as useful as
paint, or a pen.

so paint,
write,
create,
rise.

here's a song for you: it's the spaces people make inside themselves for the people they love and the hollow sounds they make when they're empty.

it took me so long to finally be able to grasp the idea that some people we meet can miss being important to us by just an inch, or a heartbeat...

because if only in another time in space or in a slight rip of our dimension could we have fallen into each others arms at full speed ahead.

but right here, right now, we are just two trains going in different directions that passed each other in just a quick, but powerful moment and what could have been possible… *is just a what if.*

[could we be perfect even for a moment before we are nothing forever?]

note to self: you only want that because you think it'll make you feel better. here you are again trying to stuff your wounds with the paper hands of strangers that you know will catch into flames eventually.

all i ever wanted to do... all i have been doing
for three books is trying to write a poem as
beautiful as you.

i thought i forgave you but i was just afraid of
the wrath and of the power of my anger. a power
that sets a flame within the pages of these books.

i wanted to haunt you not forgive you.

[the heart of a poet]

let me die still loving and in so, i’ll never die.

i don't know where home is anymore.
i've become a helpless child who keeps building sandcastles over and over again even when the shore keeps washing it away...

this homesickness,
this promise of happiness,
this chasing of moons,

desperate, trying to find a place for my restless soul to rest, a place where my heart is full,

but every time i almost grab it and taste it...

it disappears into thin air.

[homeless]

i first experienced pain at a very young age. when i was eight years old my whole world as i knew it shattered right before my very own eyes. the pain i was experiencing made me create this safe space in my mind, a safe haven, my own little world where no one could ever hurt me ever again. a world where no monsters or corruption could enter. children are powerful in that way. Resilient and adaptable to horrors. i found refuge in flowers, lost myself in books, in the hum of a song, in the grass tickling my feet and in the purples and oranges in every sunset. pain could of dictated my life but i gave it no power. my biggest act of rebellion wasn't now, it was at the tender age of eight years old. this cruel world wanted me to stumble, cry, yell and hate back, to be shaken up by pain but i can barely hear that from where i'm at, because to this day i've kept my little safe haven, my little world in my mind. hate has no power here. my power is in my love. i rebel quietly, softly, with a pen and paper in one hand and a flower in another.

lost a lot of idols in 2020 but i gained more knowledge and more wisdom.

[i call it balance]

a song for the birthday allergic:

after twenty eight years i finally realized that it was never that i hated my birthday or growing older—

i hated mandatory attention, forced love and material gifts.

this year i want to keep my circle small and celebrate my gratitude for one more trip around the sun.

i want to sit beneath the moon and tell her "i think i'm starting to understand."

[the december language of the eternal grief]

to my rebellious beautiful souls who've found this book: read more books, be cultured and smart. so many people have fought and died for our right to read. for when you read, you will unlock your true freedom.

remember your mind is a weapon to fight, a shield to defend.

take good care of it. keep it sharp and polished.

don't ever let the precious treasure that is the mind go to waste.

i used to find power in the fire of chaos...

now i find it in the grass and breeze, it sounds a lot like coming home.

[every year i sink deeper into myself]

as much as i love conspiracy theories, my favorite theory is the one about how many times could a heart bend and break until it's heard.

[just a theory]

i never would of thought that you were going to
make here, into this book.

i never thought you were going to tear me apart.

i could of sworn you would never make it here in
between these pages where old lovers come to die,

i never would of thought this was how we would say
goodbye.

[congratulations i finally turned you into poetry]

you need anything to be inspired,
to bring art to life.

you don't need a muse, you don't need tragedy.

you don't need tragedy despite it being all you've ever known.

tragedy allowed you to grow,
but now you're free.

[the end of an era]

when i die, when it's my time to leave this earth,
when i finally leave from myself, when i've become
too tired to continue...

just promise me this,

lay my body to rest in a beautiful field of
flowers.

no tombstone, no cemetery, no crying,
just give me flowers.

[flowers and philosophies]

ancient soul,
dark,
romantic,
thrilling,

natures bride.

[and most importantly, love filled lungs]

be right back, in the forest searching for portals to other dimensions.

[god is an alien]

the end of a trilogy--

it's never good-bye, but a see you later. thank you for going on this journey with me. always.

xx k.t.

visit karinatavares.com

other books by karina—

flowers in the winter
sonder

www.ingramcontent.com/pod-product-compliance
Ingram Content Group UK Ltd.
Pitfield, Milton Keynes, MK11 3LW, UK
UKHW040028200726
13854UKWH00001B/406